HARLECH LLEYN

The history of south-west Gwynedd

Michael Senior

Printed and published by:
Gwasg Carreg Gwalch, Capel Garmon, Llanrwst.
Tel: Betws-y-Coed 261

Text © 1988 Michael Senior

ISBN: 0-86381-086-1

*Cover: Old print supplied and painted by
Olwen Caradog Evans*

GWASG CARREG GWALCH

2. *Sarn Badrig* — *a straight bank of stones 13-14 miles long, thought by some to be the remains of Cantre'r Gwaelod's dykes.*

A LAND OF MYTHS

THE evidence available to the archeologist is essentially limited; it consists of things which happen to have been durable enough to have survived. These can provide only a partial picture of the past, and it may help to give this substance if we see it in the context of a record perhaps even more durable and persistent, the remains of the oral tradition.

The stories collected in the book known as 'The Mabinogion' were written down during the Middle Ages, but tell of events of a much earlier period, and may well have been passed down by storytellers from times now effectively lost to us in every other way. They became distorted in the process, of course. But through them we may gain at least an insight into the relative early importance of different areas, and nowhere is this effect more striking than in the Harlech area and Lleyn. This part of the coast of south-west Gwynedd is exceptionally rich in traditional tales.

Some of these indicate clearly that the coastline has changed. Inundation stories are universal, but the fact that they have a powerful symbolic function does not mean that the inundations to which they have become attached did not occur, and we must at least consider the possibility that not one, but two lost lands lie off this coast.

One of these is said to be in what is now Caernarfon Bay, south-west of the spit, Morfa Dinlle, which forms the mouth of the Menai Strait. A reef of stones known as Caer Arianrhod forms its visible evidence, marked as such on some maps, and located a short distance offshore between Llandwrog and Clynnog (1). It has been recorded and remarked on since the early 17th century, and investigations in the early 20th concluded variously that it was an ancient stone circle, or the ruins of masonry, or (perhaps rather more realistically) a denuded 'drumlin', a lump of land deposited by a glacier from which the encroaching sea has removed the soil, leaving the boulders. At low tide it can be seen from the coast nearby, and stands out as a line of stones of some straightness and evenness, a larger stone in the middle rising above them.

The name means 'Arianrhod's Castle', and it is clearly the place referred to in the story of 'Math, son of Mathonwy', in which the magician Gwydion brought his nephew, Lleu Llaw Gyffes, to confront the latter's malicious mother, Arianrhod. It is interesting to note that 'Caer Arianrhod', as well as being this submerged group of stones, is the Welsh term for the constellation known as the Corona Borealis, and this connection relates Arianrhod directly to the Greek goddess Ariadne, whose silver circlet became that group of stars in Greek mythology. We thus perhaps have here an early religious site, the home or 'castle' of the local version of a pan-European goddess.

3. Coastal iron-age fort of Dinas Dinlle.
4. Llandanwg church, partially submerged in sand-dunes.

A LAND OF MYTHS

Such shadowy figures as the wizard Gwydion seem to move in a past deeply remote from us. Slightly nearer to history is the story of the second drowned country, of Cantref y Gwaelod, which tells of events which are supposed to have taken place in the sixth century, the period of small kingdoms which followed the Roman withdrawal. The story itself is of considerable antiquity.

At that time, it says, the area off the coast between Harlech and Barmouth, now part of Cardigan Bay, was a rich and fertile land. Being lowlying (the name means 'Bottom hundred') it needed constant defence against the sea, and the story relates that one night the man in charge of the floodgates, being drunk, neglected to close them. The idyllic kingdom went under the waves.

The supposed corroboration of this tale lies visible off the coast midway between Harlech and Barmouth. It is a bank of stones called Sarn Badrig (2) which starts from a point about a mile offshore and runs southwestwards for thirteen to fourteen miles. During the great period of coastal shipping in the last century it was notorious as a navigational hazard. Its name, translated as St Patrick's causeway, carries a further legend that it was the means which the saint used to cross between Ireland and Wales. The name 'Badrig' provides an alternative derivation, which may be only word-play, since it could be interpreted as 'boat-ripper'.

What makes this reef remarkable, and obliges us to consider the theory that it is manmade, is that for all its considerable length it is almost exactly straight. There are other such banks in the sea in this area, but none so dramatic as Sarn Badrig. Whether natural or not, they certainly indicate that there was dry land once where there is now sea.

There is no doubt that the coastline is constantly changing, and that both land and sea have risen and sunk at various times. Under the sand at many spots around our coast, and in some places exposed at low tide on the shore, there are fossilised forests. Illustrating graphically the change since Iron Age times, half the ring fort of Dinas Dinlle, once forming a promontory, has now gone into the sea (3). Indeed the change is faster than that in places. The church at Llandanwg (4), not far from Sarn Badrig, gets periodically immersed in sand. The exchange between land and water is, moreover, a two-way one. A plain now stretches for some three-quarters of a mile seawards from what was once the watergate of Harlech castle — though in this case, as we shall see, the situation is complicated by the change in course of a river. The rock of Harlech (clearly a place of importance long before Edward I built his fine fortress there) (27) is described in the Mabinogion story of 'Branwen' as "overlooking the sea", and clearly that feature would have added to its strategic usefulness.

The mention of Harlech in the story of Branwen is further evidence of the religious significance of this area in early times, since it specifies that it was a court of Brân, a personage who, behind the humanised character of the tale, is recognisable as an ancient European god, perhaps a river deity.

5. Twrog's stone, against the wall of Maentwrog church.

6. Marks of ancient structures can be seen over a wide area around Tomen y Mur.

A LAND OF MYTHS

Brân it was who owned the cauldron of rebirth, which was one of the early versions of the magic vessel which developed into the Holy Grail.

The story tells how those of Brân's followers who survived the final battle between the British and the Irish fled southwards with his severed head, evidently a magical talisman, and paused on the rock of Harlech for a feast which lasted seven years. The presence of the head counteracted the effect of the passage of time.

The area, in fact, is exceptionally rich in magical and mystical associations, all specifically located. The wizard Gwydion, who brought his protegé Lleu Llaw Gyffes to Caer Arianrhod, had previously defeated Pryderi, the king of South Wales, by magic, on the sands of the Glaslyn estuary below Maentwrog. The fallen king was buried there, and the story particularly mentions his grave. There is indeed a prehistoric stone set into the wall of the church at Maentwrog (5), (itself perhaps built there because of the spot's prior sacredness), which reminds one of those sometimes to be found in burial chambers, a rounded monolith known as Twrog's stone.

The sequel of the story of Gwydion and Llew, as told in 'Math, son of Mathonwy', is specific to this area also, since the young hero set up court at Tomen y Mur, a Roman camp with an impressive and mysterious mound, which overlooks the lake of Trawsfynydd, at the very edge of the moorland (6). There his unfaithful wife Blodeuwedd tricked him into revealing how he might be slain, and her lover killed him on the bank of the river Cynfal. This tumbling stream flows strongly down its valley still, crossed by the road on which one ascends from Ffestiniog to Trawsfynydd. It was on that river also that Lleu, resurrected by Gwydion's magic, took his revenge (7). Magnanimously he allowed his rival to protect himself with a stone, but Lleu's spear passed through both the stone and the lover. "And there the stone is, on the bank of the Cynfael river in Ardudwy, and the hole through it."

His fickle wife Blodeuwedd was turned by Gwydion into an owl, and in that form bemoans her fate to this day, while her maidens fled from the court at Tomen y Mur on Gwydion's approach, and, looking backwards in fear, walked into the moorland lake above Ffestiniog and drowned, giving it the name it still bears, Llyn Morwynion, 'the maidens' lake' (8).

The story of the inundation of Cantref y Gwaelod has a sequel too, which tells how Elffin, the prince who had thus lost his inheritance, fished a weir on the river Dovey, south of our present area, where he found an abandoned child, who turned out to be the inspired bard Taliesin.

Taliesin and Gwydion are perhaps the two most powerful figures in the original native British mythology, and for them both to have associations with this area would in itself mark it out as being of special mystical importance, even if this coincidence were not reinforced by such a wealth of other material. The evidence in the world of ideas for this area's early religious significance is supported also by substantial remains in the world of stone.

EARLY INHABITANTS

IF Ardudwy and Lleyn seem to us remote now, it is because we are adjusted to thinking of the basic means of travel as being across land. In those circumstances they are certainly cut off from the great world, by the very physical obstacle of a major mountain range. Quite the reverse, however, has been from time to time the case, and particularly in the early phases of man's civilisation the primary mode of transport was by sea. Viewed in the light of that, these mild coastal areas lie at a prime spot on a major seaway. Much of their prehistory may be explained at once by that simple fact.

One such feature which would otherwise be puzzling is the density of population from Neolithic, through Bronze Age and Iron Age times, which the prehistoric remains in this area clearly imply. Among the earliest monuments in Britain are the various styles of chambered tombs, and there are no less than six of these within a five-mile radius in the area of Harlech. Similarly the centre of the Lleyn peninsula boasts, as we shall see, an equivalent number of Iron Age forts.

The chambered tombs, dating from about 2,500 B.C., are of a type which indicates connections with Ireland and southern Britain, particularly the Cotswold area, and it makes much sense to see this as a stopping point (based perhaps on the natural harbour formed by the mouth of the Artro river, near Llandanwg) between these two major Neolithic centres. The tombs here are of the 'portal' type, best examined perhaps in the two very fine examples which lie behind the school at Dyffryn Ardudwy (9).

Now two separate chambers, these are still surrounded by the remains of the vast mound of stones which originally united them in a single monument. The form, once one looks for it, is clear. A pair of uprights slightly higher than the others forms what appears to be a doorway at the eastern end of the chamber, their flat sides facing each other; a universal characteristic of this feature is that the apparent doorway is then blocked, in a way which must have been permanent and intrinsic to the design, by a slightly lower stone set across the gap between them to form the cross-piece, on a plan, of the letter H. Since this feature means that the portal cannot have been used as such, its nature must be symbolic or conventional. A result of the greater height of the portal stones is that the capstone slopes downwards slightly towards the west.

The capstones are normally smooth and flat underneath, but rounded and rough on top, suggesting perhaps that their underside was intended to be seen, by people entering the tomb, but that their exterior would have been covered. Indeed the tombs were always intended to be built over by a mound of stones, and the extent of such a covering can be seen in the Dyffryn example. The great field enclosures of the 19th century led to an enormous amount of wall-building, as may be plainly seen on the slopes and foothills around, and we know by comparing 18th-century

12. The so-called Roman Steps, a pack-horse track above Cwm Bychan.

9. *A fine pair of chamber-tombs at Dyffryn Ardudwy.*
13. *Porth Dinllaen, at one time intended to be the port for Ireland.*

EARLY INHABITANTS

descriptions and drawings with what may now be seen that a large quantity of the covering stones has in most instances been removed.

The tombs had in any case been robbed and damaged at earlier dates, and not much of interest has ever been found within them. When the Dyffryn chambers were investigated archeologically in 1962-3 some small pieces of Neolithic pottery were found, which helped to date the structure and indicate its phases of development. The cairns and chambers of the Carneddau Hengwm complex, a little to the south, have similarly been much damaged, but it remains impressive for its size and its situation (10).

Those mentioned here are by no means the only chambered tombs or cairns in our area, simply the best examples. There are fine ones too at Cefnamwlch and in the area of Rhiw on the Lleyn peninsula, and remnants of another chambered cairn at Cors y Gedol, the ancient house near Dyffryn which was the home of the Vaughan family.

A small piece of evidence that perhaps at one time more was to be seen at sacred sites such as these lies behind a pew at the back of the nearby church of St Peter at Llanbedr (11). It is a modest piece of stone, but it bears an image which connects it with the great burial mounds of the Boyne valley in Ireland and with many other ancient sites in Europe, the incised spiral figure which may well represent the endless cycles of decay and renewal.

The foothills and the range which blocks the hinterland of the Harlech coast from the Trawsfynydd valley are seamed with trackways. From the frequency along those of cairns and standing stones it seems that they must have been there at least as early as the Bronze Age. The well-known 'Roman Steps' (12), above Cwm Bychan, no doubt lie on such a route, ascending as they do to the natural pass of Bwlch Tyddiad. The steps themselves probably owe their origin not to the Romans but to the use of this way as a pack-horse track in the Middle Ages, and probably before.

A quite remarkable area, probably associated with a prehistoric trackway, lies above Llandecwyn, to the north of Harlech, in a valley rising to a point called Bryn Cader Faner, where a striking cairn is sited on a prominent knoll. Here the whole land has a deep feeling of undisturbed ancientness. The ground is littered with signs of prehistoric works, cairns, circles, banks, walls, some clustered, some magnificently alone, many (neatly built and yet not prominently placed) defying explanation.

The traditional view of the change from one culture to another, which is visible to us from the style of the remains, sees the arrival of new people in the form of invasion. Although no doubt such events occurred, it may be too simple a way of explaining change, and possibly we should also imagine the continuous spreading, like a tide creeping up the beach, of new influences, new discoveries, innovations of technique. In any case the development of the use of metal tools enabled an advance from the early farming culture of the late stone age into a more settled and structured period which we know (for this reason) as the Bronze Age.

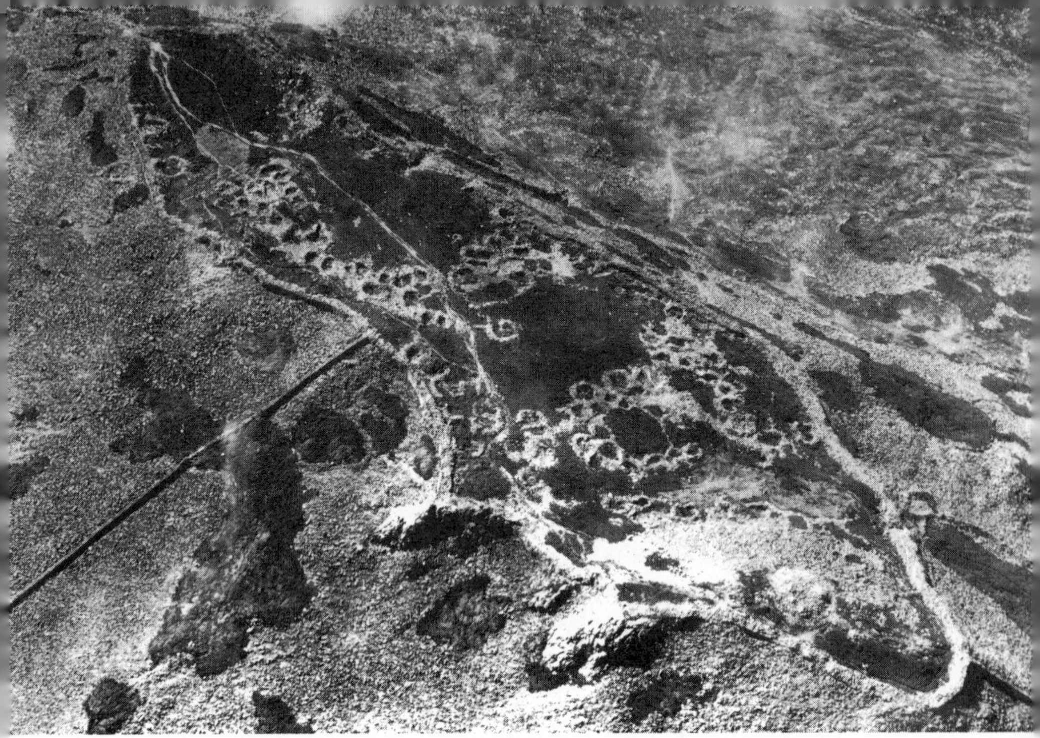

14. Tre'r Ceiri, iron-age hillfort on the summit of Yr Eifl.

Section of the
wall-walk.

Hut inside the
enclosed area.

EARLY INHABITANTS

To that period of expansion and development we owe many of the burial cairns and standing stones, but still there is no clear evidence of the remains of dwellings. When we move forward further to the period based on the use of iron, a time specifically associated with the culture which came to be called Celtic, the matter is very different. Literally hundreds of the huts which were their homes can be seen in the Lleyn peninsula alone.

To generalise about our area, it seems that the Harlech hinterland, the land known historically as Ardudwy, was a centre of activities in the Neolithic and Bronze Ages, and the Lleyn more important in the Iron Age. Just as six neolithic tombs stand within a few miles of each other in Ardudwy, so Lleyn boasts a surprising cluster of prime examples of Iron Age forts. From Dinas Dinlle in the north, on the coast near Llandwrog, via Tre'r Ceiri, Porth Dinllaen and Garn Boduan to Garn Fadrun, is altogether seventeen miles, and these were the equivalent in their time of major towns.

As we remarked in the previous chapter, only half of the ring fort of Dinas Dinlle (3) is left. The rest has fallen into the sea. Standing on top of it you can see on the beach below the rounded, even stones which once composed it. It is a remarkably large and steep mound in this generally flat, low-lying area, and must always have been a prominent landmark.

Legend, and its name, connect the fort with Lleu Llaw Gyffes, whom we met in connection with his mother's seat, Caer Arianrhod, which lies not far offshore from here. Gwydion and Lleu are described as walking on the seashore near Aber Menai, and the fort is specifically named as the place where Lleu grew up. Dates for such structures are vague, and to say that it belongs to the Iron Age places its occupation from perhaps the early years B.C. up to the period of the Roman invasion. Finds of Roman coins indicate that it was still in use in the 2nd and 3rd centuries A.D.

These ringed forts are normally on hilltops, and Dinlle is unusual in having been built on what was probably a glacial deposit overlooking a convenient landing place. Its neighbour at Dinllaen, we shall see, is in a similar position, and both perhaps remind us more of the promontory forts of Ireland than of North Wales' more common hillfort version.

The fact that Dinlle (like several other forts) has a double rampart — an outer wall halfway up its slope, an inner one surrounding its broad top — is seen by some as evidence of two periods of use, a rebuilding or improvement being carried out after the fort had been taken, or occupied after being abandoned, by an invading force.

No legendary traditions attach to the similar fort at Dinllaen (13), but its position and style make it seem likely to have been the work of the same people. It too overlooks a convenient landing place. In this case full use is made of the isthmus site, since the fort occupies the narrow neck of the peninsula. It has been partly damaged by the construction of the golf course and by the cutting of a road down to the buildings on the shore. Due to the occupation of the whole headland by the golf club, Porth Dinllaen as a whole

15. Nant Gwrtheyrn, now a Welsh-learners' language centre.
16. Garn Boduan. Inset: Hut circles in Garn Boduan.

EARLY INHABITANTS

is not accessible to the public by car, but when the tide is out there is a pleasant walk along the beach.

These remains, and indeed almost everything of the period which one finds in North Wales, seem sparse and modest when one comes to Tre'r Ceiri, the 'town of the giants' (14). It stands on the easternmost of the three peaks known as the Rivals, a name adapted to a Welsh form as Yr Eifl. Finds here have indicated a period of use at least up to the end of the 4th century A.D., starting from sometime in the mid-second. These are all we have evidence for, but the presence of an apparently bronze-age cairn at the summit of the hill which the ramparts enclose indicates earlier uses of the site. The point which is of interest is that the occupation of all these forts overlapped, and whether they were inhabited by the same group of people or by groups of different origins there remains a compelling conclusion from their size and their proximity: in and around the 3rd century A.D. Lleyn was remarkably densely populated.

Tre'r Ceiri is huge. The buildings themselves are not giant-like, nor even particularly large for their period, but the extent of the site is certainly impressive. Within its 950-feet by 340-feet enclosure there are the remains of some 150 huts. The features that make Tre'r Ceiri unusual are this extensiveness and the state of preservation of its structures. It looks in fact quite recently built, perhaps temporarily vacated. Whether this is because of a higher quality of construction than usual, or because the remoteness of its position has made it less vulnerable to interference it is hard to say. Certainly many lower forts have suffered from the effects of later works and of farming. On the other hand Tre'r Ceiri does give the impression of being somehow better built: the faced walls of the huts, the battlements with, on the seaward side, their wall-walk still in place, they all display a confidence on the part of their makers in the perfection of their skills.

Its state of preservation also makes it particularly valuable as an illustration of how such Iron Age structures would have looked when they were new: the wall-walks and the incurving walls of the huts are features to bear in mind when visiting more ruined forts.

The fact that Tre'r Ceiri stands around the summit of a steeply-sided mountain of 1,500 feet is sufficient to ration the number of people who see it. It is, in fact, well worth the effort. Not only is there the experience of stepping into the world of a millennium and a half ago, but there is also a view of a great deal of North Wales.

One of the most remarkable things in this area crowded with impressive artefacts is a natural feature. Nant Gwrtheyrn, however, has a tenuous but appealing link with history (15). Its name connects it with the high-king of the Britons, Vortigern, who is blamed by early historians for facilitating the Saxon invasion. It is a well-established tradition that when the situation deteriorated the high-king fled to North Wales. At Dinas Emrys, above Beddgelert, he is said to have tried to build a castle. This

EARLY INHABITANTS

startlingly steep and isolated ravine, 'Vortigern's valley', was his second and last place of refuge.

There is some indication in the lore that after his failure, and in effect capitulation, arising as they did out of error or folly, Vortigern was in need of protection against his own people as well as the invaders. He could not have picked a better spot to ensure isolation from the whole world than Nant Gwrtheyrn. Hanging valleys on enclosing cliffs rear vertiginously over a plainly exclusive zone. You look down into it, but the height and the steepness discourage entry.

There are as it happens many signs of ancient habitation in the valley and around it, although the mound called Castell Gwrtheyrn is probably natural. Until about 1700 there apparently stood on this outcrop a stone burial chamber complete with its covering mound, known as Bedd Gwrtheyrn, 'Vortigern's grave'. According to Pennant, writing in the 1770's, the locals excavated it themselves and discovered the bones of a tall man in a stone coffin.

There are early hut circles and long huts in and around the valley, and when Pennant visited it it was farmed by three families, so that in spite of its obvious inhospitableness it seems to have been inhabited continuously from prehistory. During the last century it became a quarrying village, and as the quarry industry declined its isolation led to gradual depopulation until its few houses stood empty. In more recent times this rather unreal place has been acquired by a trust to form the National Language School, providing a successful centre for the teaching of Welsh — an appropriate recompense, perhaps, for Vortigern's ancient mistake.

Five miles from Tre'r Ceiri is a fort of a similar size, Garn Boduan, also on a steep high hill (16). Most visible of the remains here is the small citadel-like fort on the summit, of Roman or sub-Roman date and apparently an addition to the main compound, which itself falls into two periods represented by its two distinct ramparts. These apparently enclose the remains of 170 huts, clusters of which are easy to see on the southern edge of the plateau. The fort is undoubtedly large and has an extensive view over the coastal plain, a breathtaking spread of field patterns and lanes, with the headlands of Penrhyn Nefyn and Porth Dinllaen on one side and the hills of the peninsula stretching away on another. Although some of the huts are unusually large, they are not as impressive or prominent as those of Tre'r Ceiri.

Less than four miles separates Garn Boduan from Lleyn's other notable hillfort. Right down the end of the peninsula, Garn Fadrun is impressive for itself, its situation and eminence, rather than for its structures (17). The enclosed area of the round mountain's flat summit is in all about 26 acres, and if anything feels larger. There are signs of the remains of a bronze-age cairn, as at Tre'r Ceiri, indicating perhaps that almost every summit had a burial of that time; the south-western area particularly is thick

EARLY INHABITANTS

with the stones of huts and structures, but none well-preserved; an inner, and apparently older wall again indicates two different periods of occupation; on the summit (as at Garn Boduan) are the walls of a later structure, in this case probably medieval. It might not have been worth the trip for the experience of these things, but in one respect Garn Fadrun is pre-eminent. It would be worth a much harder climb to gain the benefit of such a view.

Struck out at the end of Wales yet surrounded by its branching coastline, Garn Fadrun provides a kind of summary of all that is most remarkable about this extraordinary landscape. The heaped mountains of Snowdonia roll on one side into their banks of cloud. The estuaries and their surrounding foothills step southwards on another. Far across the bay we look to South Wales, where the Pembrokeshire coast juts expansively into the Irish Sea. The coast of Anglesey and Holy Island and sometimes, beside and beyond them, the Irish hills, enclose the remaining horizon. Such a spread and such variety of view can surely be found in few other places.

17. Garn Fadrun.

THE NEW ERA

THE Roman Empire relied largely on land transport, their chief weapon being their powerful network of roads. Along these armies could march at speed and messages be relayed. In spite of the difficulties they penetrated North Wales as far as Caernarfon, formed a camp at the edge of the moor above Trawsfynydd (6) and another, quite recently discovered, at Dolbenmaen at the peninsula's neck; but they did not apparently attempt to colonise Lleyn, and their presence is mainly transitory in the foothills of Ardudwy.

The camp at Dolbenmaen may have been a posting point on the route between the major fort of Segontium at Caernarfon, and the auxiliary outpost at Tomen y Mur. The latter (mentioned already in connection with the Mabinogion story in which it was the seat of the hero Lleu Llaw Gyffes) is of some importance, since it was the point at which the road from Segontium and that from Canovium in the Conwy Valley joined up on their route southwards to the South Wales centre Mordunum, now Carmarthen.

At Tomen y Mur there are extensive remains to be seen, now mainly in the form of grass banks, including the area of an amphitheatre, a little way from the main fort. The most conspicuous feature is the mound or 'tomen' which gives the place its name, thought to be the motte of a medieval castle, which would have been a wooden structure on its top, probably built by an English earl attempting invasion. The most striking quality of the site is its extreme exposure, a bleakness and lack of shelter which must have tested the hardiness of its Roman garrison.

When the Romans left a long period of unsettled conditions resulted for which records are sparse. Though we know of this as the 'Dark Ages' it must not be assumed to be by any means empty of events. In this part of North Wales raids from across the Irish Sea were the initial problem, and we may guess that in places the ineffectiveness of resistance to these led to colonisation. There may indeed have been an element of earlier affinity. Ireland and the Lleyn are after all within sight of one another.

Elsewhere in Britain the trouble came not from the west but from the continent of Europe. Although it took some time to penetrate into this fastness, its effects came ahead of it.

One major change which had come about during the sub-Roman period was the spread of Christianity. In its early western form this took a monastic nature, small communities of religious people being based on a sacred settlement under the auspices of a missionary leader, whose name often survives in church dedications as an area's local saint.

Such communities favoured remoteness, and that factor became more important as Saxon raids on Christian sites in the border country and mid-Wales uprooted and intimidated the monks who had previously flourished there. Remoteness is one quality the Lleyn peninsula had to offer, once the focus of danger had shifted eastwards, and nowhere is it

18. Bardsey Island.

18. Bardsey: remains of the abbey and the farm buildings.
19. Clynnog Fawr, the main church on the pilgrim route.

THE NEW ERA

better exemplified than on the island of Bardsey (18).

As early as the beginning of the 6th century St Cadfan had founded a monastery there. As troubles elsewhere increased it became the refuge of other holy men, and dispossessed communities of monks flocked there during the 7th century. Thus it was that it came to be regarded as an especially sacred place.

Giraldus Cambrensis (who toured North Wales with Archbishop Baldwin in 1188) records that the island was remarkably free from disease, and says that "very many bodies of saints are said to be buried there". It was evidently after his time that the legend grew that the number of these was 20,000. To be the burial place of a single saint gave a religious spot much prestige, and qualified it as the destination of pilgrimage. To be the reputed burial-place of 20,000 raised this island to a unique position, and in terms of medieval merit three pilgrimages to Bardsey were the equivalent of one to Rome.

Hence it was that a pilgrim route grew up, as influential on the area then as a tourist itinerary is today. A number of substantial churches grew along the route, where pilgrims might pause for both devotion and sustenance. Starting with Clynnog Fawr (19), the largest and greatest of these, we have a chain stretching in easy stages: Llanaelhaearn, Pistyll, Nefyn, Edern, Tudweiliog, Penllech, Llangwnnadl, Aberdaron. Some of these are truly notable.

Clynnog itself is famous for its magnificence, a late-15th century building largely extended in the early 16th. It is said to have been founded by St Beuno, patron of many North Wales churches, in the 7th century, and a 16th-century chapel linked to the main church by a passage encloses the supposed spot of the original foundation. Beuno himself was said to have been buried there in the late 7th century. The monastery which he founded served the pilgrim travellers through the Middle Ages, and remained as a religious community even after the Dissolution of the Monasteries.

Beuno was a saint associated with healing, and a story connecting him with St Winifred's Well at Holywell shows him as being able to cure even decapitation. Winifred had her head cut off by the local king, and Beuno successfully stuck it back on. St Winifred (as she then became) went on to live another 15 years. Pennant records that on his visit to Clynnog in the 1770's Beuno's tomb (now no longer apparent) was a resort of the sick:

> In the midst is the tomb of the saint, plain, and altar-shaped. Votaries were wont to have great faith in him, and did not doubt but that by means of a night's lodging on his tomb, a cure would be found for all diseases. It was customary to cover it with rushes, and leave on it till morning sick children, after making them first undergo ablution in the neighbouring holy well; and I myself once saw on it a feather bed, on which a poor paralytic from

20. *St. Beuno's church at Pistyll. Inset: 12th century font with ancient Celtic pattern.*
21. *The church of St. Gwynhoedl at Llangwnnadl.*

THE NEW ERA

Merioneddshire had lain the whole night, after undergoing the same ceremony.

The church, says Pennant, "is the most magnificent structure of its kind in North Wales", and it would be hard to disagree. He tells us also of the legend that all calves and lambs born with 'Beuno's mark', "a certain natural mark in the ear", were delivered as offerings to the church, being sold by the churchwardens to effect repairs. The custom apparently continued in his day. The medieval chest in which they kept the funds in the meantime, 'Beuno's chest', may still be seen in the church.

Another Beuno church, but very different in style, is that at Pistyll (20). The area of the farm by the church was a hospice for pilgrims, and the monks grew hops and fruit in the surrounding area and, in the healing tradition inherited from Beuno, medicinal herbs, some of which still survive in the churchyard.

St Beuno's church at Pistyll is evidence of the power of simplicity, its old stonework and plain rectangular plan creating an atmosphere of peace and harmony as effectively as might any lounder statement. Its present structure is largely original, probably dating from the 12th century with a slight eastern extension in the 15th. A fine font of 12th-century date bears a Celtic image of endlessness, intertwined strands similar to those of the 'endless knot'. Until it was slated in the last century the church was thatched, and the rope-holes by which the thatched roof was secured can be seen in its timbers. The entrance to an earlier form of the building — perhaps even that founded in the 7th century by Beuno — may be seen in the form of steps jutting from the base of the south wall. A corner-stone of this older building is also visible in the eastern part of the north wall, and another early feature is the lepers' window, by which lepers outside the church might see the altar and the elevation of the host.

A contrast to Pistyll again is the striking perpendicular-style church of Llangwnnadl (21). One does not expect this elevated style in something so small, associating it rather with grander structures. Here it is most effective, and gives to Llangwnnadl (a name contracted from its dedication to St Gwynhoedl) a very pleasant lightness and air of uplift. The fact that the church dates mainly from the 1520's and '30's (although its original foundation, like that of all the others in this area, is of the dark-age period) is evidence of the success and longevity of use of the pilgrim route. The two extra aisles were added to an old rectangular structure, now the central aisle, at this period, the north aisle first and the south some ten years later. These effects of the great popularity of this resting place on the journey give to the church now its most unusual shape and spaciousness.

The culmination of the journey must have been the arrival at Aberdaron, where the church of St Hywyn stands at the very edge of the shore, its graveyard protected from an aggressive sea by a strong defensive

THE NEW ERA

wall (22).

Aberdaron church is mainly of the early 16th century, though the Norman doorway is original and that part of the west wall surrounding it and the north wall adjoining are of the 12th century. The earlier pilgrims' oratory, dating back to the 6th century, the time when Cadfan (to whom St Hywyn, Aberdaron's patron, was confessor) founded the original settlement on Bardsey, would have been made of wood, and this structure, like so many others, represents part of the great programme of church-building in stone which took place in a Norman style in the settled and relatively prosperous period of the first half of the 12th century. A curious feature of St Hywyn's today is that the build-up of sand has raised the level of the surrounding churchyard so that the interior of the church seems to be below ground.

There is very little to see now on Bardsey Island (in Welsh, Ynys Enlli) itself of the great medieval monastery which must have stood there. Pennant describes an oratory and the Abbot's house, although, by then even, the religious community was a part of a distant past, Bardsey's spiritual life being "under the care of a single rustic," a place which "once afforded, during life, an asylum to 20,000 saints; and after death, graves to as many of their bodies."

The pilgrims left from a cove a little south of Aberdaron, called Porth Meudwy (23), but now the official route is from Pwllheli, from where there are organised trips during the summer in suitable weather. The island became almost depopulated, but is now returning to life as a nature reserve. The buildings there today are farms built in the 19th century; the crumbling remains of the tower of the abbey church is all that is left of the monastery (18). The early Celtic foundation had become Augustinian in the 13th century, suffered Dissolution in the 16th, and its buildings fell to ruins in the 19th century.

A lighthouse kept the island inhabited from 1821, and in the 1870's a new farming community was established by Lord Newborough, whose family owned the island for generations. The Newboroughs, descended from the Glyns, or Glynnes, of Glynllifon (24), near Llandwrog, had married into the Wynn family in about 1700, and came to be owners of a considerable spread of property. Indeed their Glynllifon estate extends over this end of the peninsula. The present house of Glynllifon (now an agricultural college) was built between 1836 and 1848 on the site of an 18th century house which had burnt down, the Newborough title, an Irish peerage, having been created in 1776.

Although early Christianity in this area undoubtedly focussed on this holy island, there is ample evidence of its independent existence elsewhere. Down the coast below Harlech, for instance, the fine little church of Llanaber (25), notable for its Early English architectural features, possesses two gravestones which date from before the 10th century. It

THE NEW ERA

stands, like Aberdaron, almost in the sea, and its neighbour at Llandanwg (4) (as has already been mentioned) is so much on the beach as to get engulfed in sand. These coastal positions indicate very early dates of foundation, since they relate to the time when the main means of travel was by sea.

22. *Aberdaron church.*

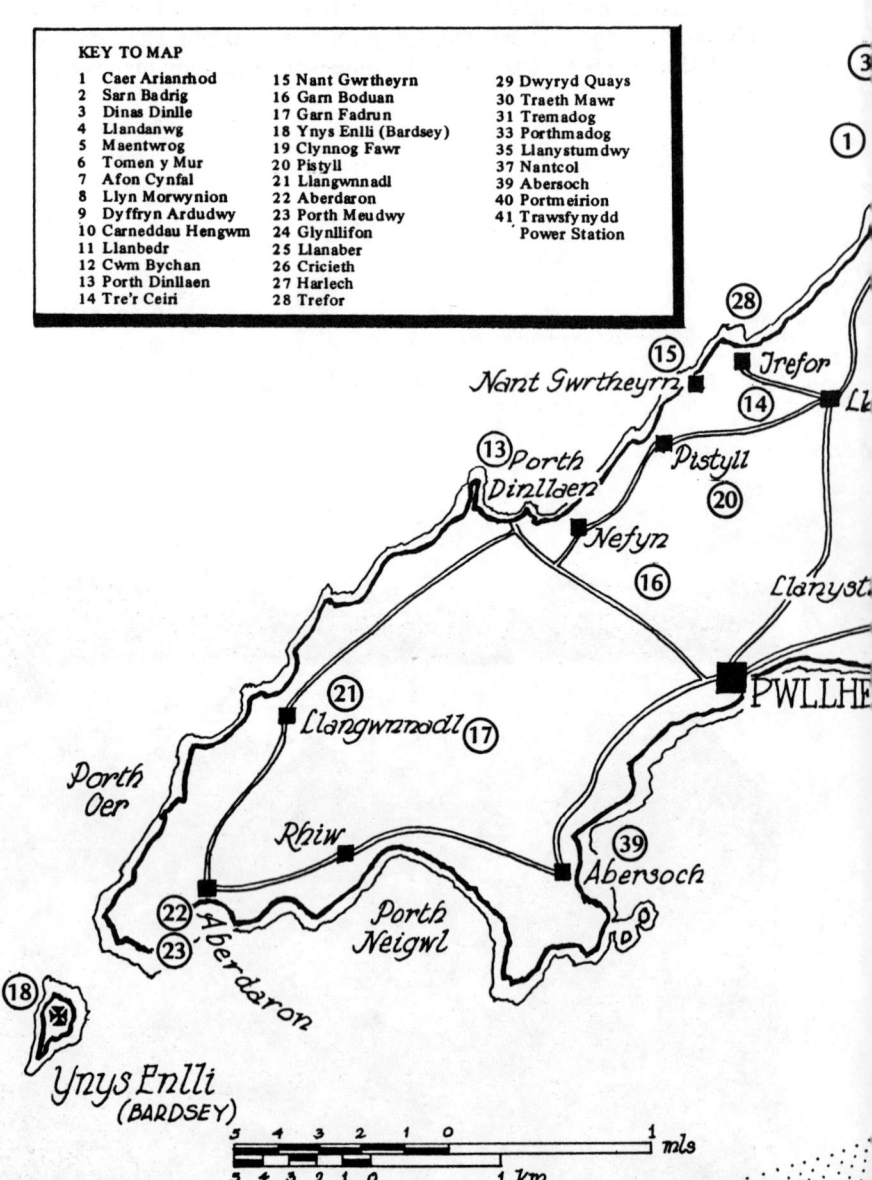

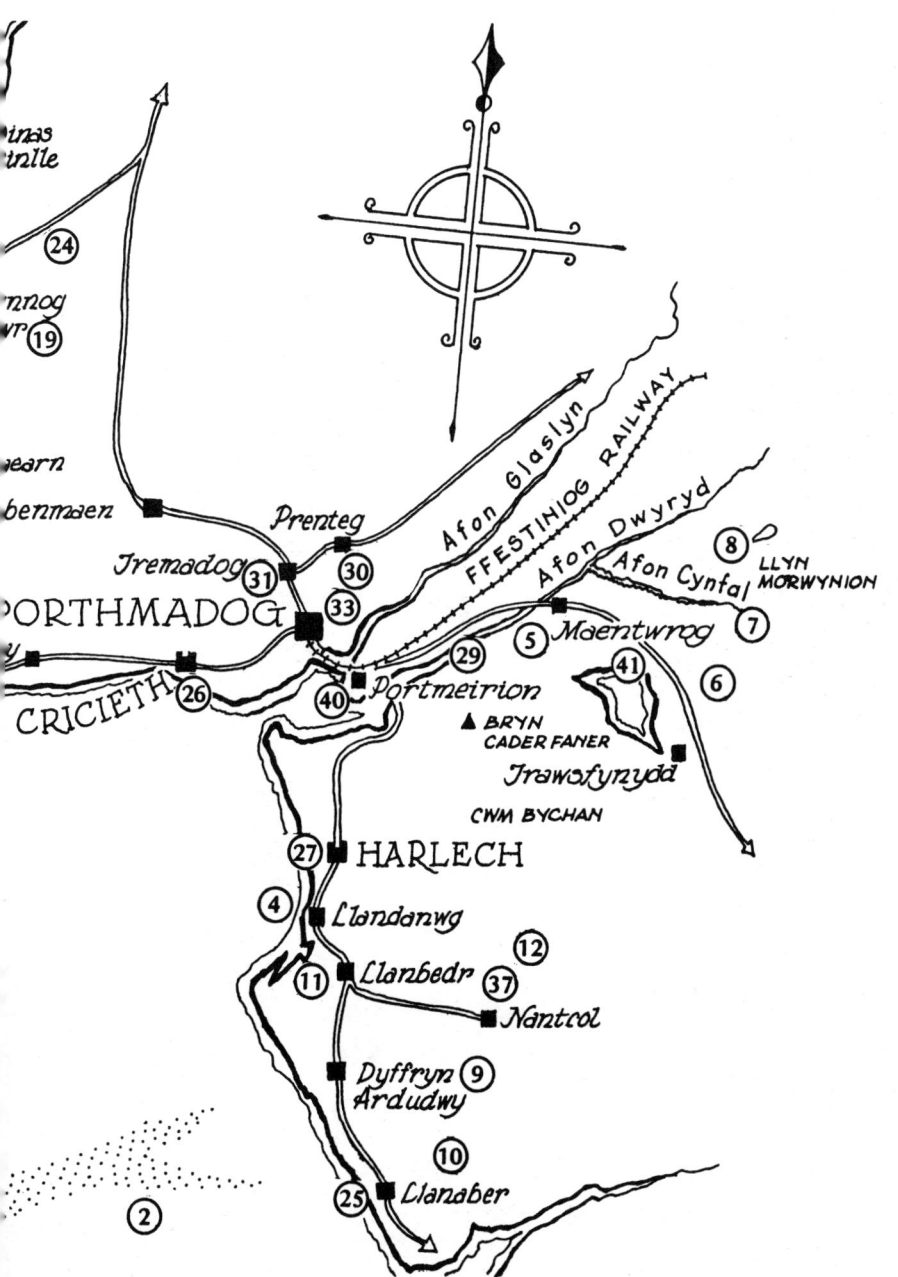

HARLECH

DURING the whole of this period, from the departure of the Romans through the early Middle Ages, North Wales had been ruled by independent princes. The castle at Cricieth, for instance, was not among those originally built by Edward I, although he strengthened it and used it (26). It was one of the seats of the princes of Gwynedd, formerly no doubt the court of the rulers of Eifionydd, and was constructed in stone in the 1230's.

The background to the situation at the close of the independent period of Wales' history is complicated by a rivalry within the ruling family. Llywelyn ab Iorwerth, known as Llywelyn the Great, ruled for more than twenty years and achieved a considerable degree of unity. When he died, in 1240, there was dispute over the succession. His elder son Gruffydd was illegitimate, though possibly favoured by the people since his legitimate son Dafydd, whom he himself wished to be heir, was half English, being the son of the Princess Joan, daughter of King John. Anticipating danger, Dafydd had Gruffydd imprisoned in Cricieth castle.

It was not the last time this secure little fortress has been put to such a use. Dafydd did not rule Wales for long, and the succession reverted to the alternative line. The next, and last, of the independent princes was Llywelyn ap Gruffydd. He similarly found it necessary to imprison a threatening rival, the heir of the South Wales dynasty, and he too used Cricieth castle. Indeed he seems to have made it his headquarters, since he wrote to Edward I from there in the 1270's. The latter came to Cricieth during his invasion of the 1280's, but decided against making it one of his major castles. He founded a borough around it, improved the inner gatehouse, but on the whole left us with a fine example of the work of the Llywelyns.

Edward and Llywelyn had started their conflict in the border country in 1277, and the tension between them reached a climax when the Welsh prince and his brother led raids on the Marches in the spring of 1282, thus breaking the rather fragile agreement which had been contrived between the two countries. Llywelyn died in a skirmish in mid-Wales at the end of that year, and Edward took advantage of the temporary confusion to launch an all-out invasion of Gwynedd, the heartland and refuge of the independent princes. He threw round the inner sanctuary of Snowdonia a great chain of castles.

The southernmost of these is Harlech (27).

Since we had cause to mention the site of Harlech castle in connection with the mythology, it is possible that this notably prominent rock was a sacred or defensive position before Edward came; but it must be said that there is no evidence of this. Harlech as we have it was one of the castles designed for Edward from scratch by Master James of St George, a Frenchman who had supervised the building of castles in Edward's other territories, and who accompanied him into Wales as master of his works

27. Inside the enclosed court of Harlech castle.

26. Cricieth castle.
27. Harlech castle.

HARLECH

there.

That Master James was a genius in his own field is clearly evident to us today. Each of Edward's North Wales castles bears its own unique style and character; yet each conforms to a rigid overall form demanded by its serious military function. Each one bears touches of symmetry and harmony, and even overt decoration, which makes it individually beautiful. Yet they all worked effectively as formidable tools of war. They are variations on a grandiose theme.

Harlech is undoubtedly the most intimate and domestic of the main three. Caernarfon is palatial and grand, Conwy somewhat intimidating in its aspect of power. Harlech is impressive from the outside, due to its splendid eminence, but in its interior it is the sort of place where one feels one could comfortably live. The great windows of its inner face look onto a securely enclosed court, giving rather the feel of a fortified manor, an atmosphere which comes as all the more of a surprise after the view of it rearing against the sky as one approaches.

Edward sited his castles with the eye of a strategist, a day's march apart and in such positions as could be supplied by sea, from his headquarters at Chester, if land communications were cut off. In view of this it is important to remember, at Harlech, that the coastline has changed, this time the land gaining from the sea. Indeed as one stands on the edge of the outer ward it is surprising that so much change could happen in the relatively short period of seven hundred years. This is thought to be partly due to the change of course of the river Dwyryd, which now meets the sea in a combined estuary with the Glaslyn some four miles further north. If the outflow of that river at that time skirted the foot of the castle rock, then Edward's harbour might well have been on that, rather than on the seashore. Certainly the Water-Gate, and the path to the castle known as 'the way from the sea' emphasise, even today, Harlech's maritime role.

Although Harlech was being built at the same time as Conwy and Caernarfon, we can see a development in style taking place which was to lead, a few years later, to the fully concentric form of Beaumaris. Harlech is in a transitional position between the older form of inner and outer wards, (developed from the keep and bailey fortresses of the earlier Middle Ages), on the one hand, in which the inner citadel is approached through the outer, and on the other the doubling-up effect displayed at Beaumaris, in which the outer ward completely encircles the inner. One can see Master James approaching this later idea at Harlech.

Once there, the castle attracted its own history. It was finished in about 1290, and immediately tested in the revolt of Madog ap Llywelyn in 1294-5. Although besieged by land, it proved the effectiveness of its water-based position, and the garrison held out against the rebels by receiving supplies by sea. Criccieth castle, refortified by Edward, proved equally effective in his service.

HARLECH

For a time there was peace, the system set up by Edward effectively ruling Wales. The death of Richard II in 1399 and the usurpation of the throne by Henry IV, however, led to a less settled situation. It was due to a dispute with a neighbour that Owain Glyndŵr found himself out of favour with the new king, and forced into the role of rebel. But evidently the time was ripe for rebellion, and all that had been lacking was a leader.

In 1401 Glyndŵr failed to take the king's castles of Caernarfon and Harlech, but he tried again in the case of Harlech in 1404. By now he had an unexpected advantage, as the garrison there had become mutinous, weakened by illness, and had started to desert. Glyndŵr seized his chance, negotiated with the pitiful remnant in the castle, and eventually bribed them with cash into surrender.

It was a chance which for a time radically affected his campaign, since he now had a headquarters. He moved his family into the pleasantly habitable security of Harlech — his wife, daughter and son-in-law, Sir Edmund Mortimer, with his four grandchildren — and for four years it was his home and capital. There, in the tradition of his ancestors at their courts, he called his Council and appointed officers. He is even said to have been crowned there, and certainly from there he concluded a treaty with the French, under the title 'Owynus Dei Gratia Princeps Wallie'.

The dream did not last. Glyndŵr could not sustain for long enough the backing of his countrymen, and when things began to look less hopeful they deserted him. In 1408 the prince and his family found themselves besieged in Harlech by a force of a thousand men. Harlech castle suffered some of the damage which it bears today in a long bombardment. Mortimer, his son-in-law, had died in the meantime, but his wife and daughter were taken prisoner. In the manner of folk heroes he himself, however, simply disappeared. He was thought to have lived for some time, outlawed and in disguise, and the date and manner of his death is still unknown.

Glyndŵr's biography and personality are essentially larger than life, and stories of a distinctly folktale nature clustered around him. Once, for instance, when he was staying with the Vaughan family in this area — an ancient line of landowners who had seats at Cors y Gedol, south of Harlech, and Nannau near Dolgellau — he was shot by his host at point-blank range. The arrow bounced off, and the attempted assassination rebounded on the hapless Vaughan, who was thought to have been immured in a hollow oak.

Harlech became prominent again in Britain's next internal struggle, the long-drawn-out Wars of the Roses, when it was a Lancastrian stronghold, and indeed held out against the victorious Yorkists longer than any other fortress. It is to this period of siege and resistance that its famous song belongs, the tune of which is traditional and finds echoes in the anthems of other nations.

Medieval castles were the most sophisticated weapon of their time, but could not anticipate the innovations of later centuries, and their

HARLECH

usefulness effectively ceased with the development of artillery. The power of gunpowder enabled the projecting of missiles over their high walls in constant bombardment, and the battering they received in these later times has left many of them in a much more ruined state than Harlech. In the Civil War of the 17th century Harlech castle was defended for the King and besieged by Oliver Cromwell's brother-in-law, a local landowner called Colonel John Jones, who later came to be one of the signatories to the King's death-warrant. His ancestral home, Maes y Garnedd, may be seen at the very end of the lane which runs up the narrow Nantcol valley.

Harlech castle withstood the siege of Colonel Jones, but eventually it surrendered to the Parliamentary army under General Mytton, in 1647. Just as it had been the last of the Lancastrian castles in Britain to fall to the Yorkists, so it was the last castle to hold out for the King against Parliament, and the Civil War was over with its surrender. That event proved to be its last military act, and from then on it has been an unoccupied ruin.

You would not think that such a quiet place could have been involved in so much history. Harlech today has few notable buildings, and indeed it seems that it never had. Pennant, in the late 18th century, describes it as being "a small and very poor town, remarkable only for its castle." Speed's map of 1610 shows only a scattering of cottages some distance from the castle. It seems that Edward I did not establish there the borough which provided a garrison of English families to administer his government, as he did at Conwy and Caernarfon. Perhaps the reason is that he had created a borough already at Cricieth nearby, to which he may have hoped to entice the essential English colony to control this area.

The town which survives under the shadow of the castle now is pleasant and successful, still small enough to have an intimate and friendly atmosphere.

QUARRIES AND SCHOONERS

WHEN Thomas Pennant made his journey through North Wales in the 1770's he recorded that the rural part of Lleyn was at that time something of a backwater. "The houses of the common people are very mean; made with clay, thatched, and destitute of chimnies." The land was largely undeveloped, grazing ground for its main agricultural product, Welsh Black cattle. It was, Pennant records, "neglected for the sake of the herring-fishery."

Pennant's implication of a conflict between the two industries, fishing and farming, it however probably an exaggeration. They have always been complementary in the Lleyn, and indeed remain so to this day. In fact the two industries in combination provided a sustantial source of income during the 18th century, although it must have been unevenly distributed if it left 'the common people' in the plight in which Pennant found them. By the end of the century Lleyn was exporting cattle to the number of about 6,000 head a year, and in the year 1747 some 5,000 barrels of herring were exported from the port of Nefyn alone. It is perhaps the ability of the region to survive by these means at a time when other areas were developing trade and industry that has kept Lleyn as rural and unaltered as it is today.

At the same time it is clear that Lleyn as a whole had deteriorated economically by the 18th century, from a relatively greater prosperity in medieval and Tudor times, probably largely because of the long neglect of its roads and the consequent barrier to communications formed by its distinctly rugged terrain.

Pwllheli and Nefyn, the two main towns and ports of the peninsula, are by no means without history. They had both been given their charters by the Black Prince in 1355, and the latter was the site chosen by Edward I for the tournament with which he celebrated his conquest of Gwynedd in 1284. Pwllheli was a fishing port of some importance by the 16th century, and is mentioned by Pennant as "the best town in this country". It had become a ship-building centre during the 18th century, and continued in this industry into the 19th until it was outstripped and in the end eclipsed by the new town of Port Madoc, by 1880.

By then several events which radically altered the balance of the area had taken place. During the first half of the 19th century the issue of the official port for Ireland was still undecided, and although investment in the harbour of Holyhead would seem to have prejudiced the decision, the problem of constructing a crossing of the Straits for a time diverted interest to the natural harbour of Porth Dinllaen (13). The route through Montgomeryshire to the Lleyn would probably have been more direct than that eventually chosen, and would have avoided the obstacle of the

34. *The Porthmadog brigantine, the 'Edward Windus', at Harburg, c. 1900.*

28. The quarry village of Trefor.
29. Slate quay on the river Dwyryd.

QUARRIES AND SCHOONERS

mountains. Even when in the 1820's the Menai Strait was successfully crossed by Telford's bridge, the matter was not finally settled, and optimistic would-be entrepreneurs continued to build suitable inns along the route, through Tremadoc and Chwilog, which they imagined the new road would take.

If all this seems surprising to us now, we must remember that Porth Dinllaen in fact had a long history already as a port for Ireland. Its rivalry with Holyhead can be traced back to the 17th century. Eventually the matter was decided officially as late as 1839, and even then the decision depended on a casting vote. Looking at it now, a tiny hamlet isolated on its headland, one's imagination is stretched by the thought of how different the scene would be, and the whole layout of North Wales' communications and settlements, if the decision had gone the other way.

In the meantime the possibility had affected other issues. Samuel Holland, whose family were to rise to prominence as developers of the Ffestiniog quarries, started quarrying stone on Yr Eifl with a view to supplying the construction of the proposed new harbour. In spite of the failure of its purpose, the quarry thrived, and a flourishing industry had developed in that area by 1850. The purpose-built village of Trefor (28), named after Holland's foreman, Trevor Jones, is the surviving evidence of this, although the quarry works themselves are now abandoned. Further quarrying outlets, each with its own pier, emerged down the inaccessible coast nearby, on the shores of the roadless hills between Trefor and Pistyll. The stone (an amalgam of quartz and porphyrite, not strictly granite) had more limited use than that of the rival works at Penmaenmawr, being sought-after for a time for monumental purposes and for making curling stones, its range of colours making it decorative as well as functional.

Although stone has been a major export along this coast at certain times, it cannot rank in importance in the area's economy in the same league as slate. The Lleyn and Harlech areas possess no great slate quarries themselves, but have inevitably been much affected historically by the vast and abundant works at Ffestiniog.

The urbanisation taking place around Britain and the newly industrial countries of Europe at the end of the 18th century led to a surge in the demand for roofing slates, for which North Wales happened to possess the ideal raw material. The price of slates doubled between the years 1798 and 1825. There had been a trade in roofing slates in North Wales since the 16th century, and the Ffestiniog quarries themselves were in operation by the end of the 18th. It was largely the arrival of the young Samuel Holland to take over the management of his father's disordered business, in 1821, that stimulated Ffestiniog's rise to prominence. By 1825 its output had increased to about 10,000 tons.

30. *Traeth Mawr as it is today.*

30. *Madock's first enbankment, near Tremadog.*

31. *Tremadog town square.*

QUARRIES AND SCHOONERS

At that time the slates were brought down a rough track on pack animals, transferred in the Vale of Ffestiniog into carts, and shipped into small boats on the river Dwyryd at a point where it is tidal, by which means they sailed down the river until it met the Glaslyn, and loaded their cargoes onto larger ships at mooring alongside the sand-dunes which form the coast between Borth-y-Gest and Morfa Bychan. The quays either side of the Dwyryd where the slates were first shipped — substantial stone structures of alternating platforms and steps — can still be seen, in many places still in excellent condition (29).

In the 1820's, however, these activities, and the area as a whole, were in the process of undergoing radical change, largely as a result of the will and determination of one man. William Alexander Madocks came from a family which owned property near Wrexham, where they were old-established landowners. His father was a successful barrister, however, and he himself was born in London, in 1773. In due course he inherited some of the Denbighshire estates and enough capital to build himself a house near Dolgellau, where he combined a vigorous social life with his legal practice in London.

Landscape improvement was a fashion of the time, and Madocks was by nature a creator, more suited to being a landscape architect and designer than a lawyer. When he started buying small farms in the neighbourhood of Penmorfa, in the 1790's, it was probably with an interest in the landscape rather than agriculture. Reclamation of the shores of the estuary had already started, as part of the widespread enclosure movement, itself caused by the agricultural revolution and consequent rise in land values. Madocks' schemes developed gradually from this, but were probably ambitious from the start.

The reclamation of Traeth Mawr (30) was not a new idea, as no doubt he knew. A scheme for reclaiming much of the estuary had been devised by Sir John Wynn (whose family originated from these parts) in 1625. Sir John was advised against it, and the project never started. Madocks however was not so easily daunted.

Part of the point of reclaiming Traeth Mawr was to do with communications, and in this the question of the port for Ireland again affected the course of events. From the days recounted by the Mabinogion onwards there had been a low-tide crossing over the sands, saving a long journey round the big inlet. A route to Porth Dinllaen from mid-Wales would avoid the problems of ferries at both Conwy and the Menai Strait, but it would come up against the equally severe difficulty of the crossing of Traeth Mawr. It was, says Pennant, "of most dangerous passage to strangers, by reason of the tides which flow here with great rapidity". The Act of Union with Ireland (effective from January 1801), which involved

QUARRIES AND SCHOONERS

Irish M.P.'s travelling regularly to Westminster, made the issue of national importance; and Madocks himself, who was Member of Parliament for Boston in Lincolnshire from 1802, helped to steer a bill through Parliament to provide the Porth Dinllaen Harbour Company, formed in 1806, with funds to build a harbour.

In the meantime his reclamation schemes were already under way. Over the course of five years he had constructed an embankment stretching from where Porthmadog now is to a point on the Beddgelert road near the hamlet of Prenteg (which may still be seen running over the fields) (30), and by 1800 he had succeeded in extending his property by this means by some 2,000 acres.

On this first area of reclamation he then built a fine small town, in an 18th century style, which he called Tremadoc (31). Although the name is undoubtedly intended to recall his own, it had the historical justification that it was traditionally the starting point of the voyage of Prince Madoc (or Madog, in its more correct form), the 12th-century Welsh explorer who was said to have been one of the first to reach America. The island from which he is reputed to have set sail is now a rocky wooded outcrop, still called after him Ynys Fadog, to the left of the road which leaves Tremadog for Porthmadog (as the names are now spelt).

Madocks improved the house above this area, Tan-yr-Allt, which he made his home. He designed both this and much of Tremadog himself, sending detailed instructions and sketches from London when he was kept there on Parliamentary business. The town hall, which housed a theatre, is much studied for its style, and the Gothic church and impressive Peniel chapel are also interesting specimens. The new town was incidentally destined to an unforeseeable claim to fame: in a small and unobtrusive house on its outskirts, now marked by a plaque, the man who was to become Lawrence of Arabia was born, in August 1888.

Below Tan-yr-Allt, near the road, Madocks brought about the first introduction of the Industrial Revolution into North Wales, in 1805, in the form of a water mill, which may still be seen, though now in disrepair. It was somewhere near this point that the old route set off across the sands.

The new land around Tremadog proved fertile, and the success of this first venture encouraged him to go further. He set about buying up the coastal lands of the estuary in order to be able to bring to reality Sir John Wynn's ambitious idea. An enclosure Bill of 1806 at first failed to gain support, and only on the third attempt did he succeed in gaining the necessary legislation for the great embankment to become a reality.

It was finished in July 1811, at a final cost of over £60,000, and left Madocks heavily in debt and greatly in need of revenue from the resulting land. This aim received a sharp set-back in February, 1812, when an

QUARRIES AND SCHOONERS

exceptional storm breached it. Help and support were raised from the whole neighbourhood, but there was still a desperate need for funds, and Madocks was now greatly financially embarrassed and hounded by creditors. His personal possessions were sold to pay off part of one enormous debt, and he was forced to transfer his lands into other ownerships and let them to his main creditor.

A surprising addition to the whole remarkable story is the arrival in the area of the poet Shelley with his young wife. Then aged only nineteen and not yet famous, he had expectations of inheritance and was romantically inclined to causes such as Madocks' reclamation scheme. He joined in the fund-raising, and subsequently became the tenant of Tan-yr-Allt. The Shelleys eventually left the area suddenly after an apparent attack on them, and the debts they left behind added to the distrust already established by those of Madocks.

In the meantime the repair of the embankment took place against all these odds. Madocks' finances revived through a fortunate marriage, and he was able to re-acquire his property and to be involved in the final phases of his grand scheme, the railway along the embankment and its destination, the quays of Port Madoc. He died before all this reached fulfilment, however, returning from a holiday in Italy, in Paris, in September 1828. His life had the heroic quality of which myth is made, and this feature extends to the story current at the time that he had not really died but returned, in disguise, like Glyndŵr, to live out the remainder of his life in obscurity.

One result of the embankment was the diversion of the River Glaslyn, and quite accidentally an effect of this was the carving out of a deep channel which made a potential new harbour. Parliamentary consent was acquired to develop this, and the construction of 'Port Madoc' was started in 1821, completed in 1824 (32). The name, now adapted to a more authentic Welsh form, was laid down in a Parliamentary Act of 1821, which gave its founder, Madocks, the right to dues, and to the appointment of a harbour-master, in recognition of his funding of the harbour works. Samuel Holland, the quarry owner, acquired a quay in the new harbour, and the development of the railway line from Ffestiniog to there was largely his scheme.

There was considerable local opposition to this, since the business of freighting slates by cart and boat on the Dwyryd provided employment. Holland however got his railway bill through Parliament and the construction started in 1833. Its thirteen miles were finished in 1836, having cost some £6,000.

It was at first a gravitational tramway, the cars pulled back up by horses which then rode down in one of them. Nearly thirty years later steam locomotives became practical, and it has been driven by steam since 1836.

32. *Port Madoc in the last century.*
33. *Porthmadog harbour now.*

By then it was transporting 76,000 tons of slate a year. In 1865 it started to carry passengers, and this of course it still does, with remarkable success. As a means of viewing North Wales' spectacular and varied scenery it has few rivals.

Port Madoc thrived in a way neither Madocks nor Holland could have predicted. The price of slate continued to rise with the building boom, and the repeal of the slate tax in 1831 boosted it further. The population of the new port rose equivalently from the 1830's to the 1850's, and it doubled again between 1851 and 1881. This led to slum conditions in some parts of the town, and in the 1850's there were problems of epidemics and overcrowding.

The sound home market for slate in the meantime enabled the opening up of exports, and Port Madoc started to ship slates to Liverpool for onward transport to Australia, and directly to the ports of Germany, where much building was also taking place at that time. Hamburg, for instance, is almost entirely roofed by Ffestiniog slate shipped from Port Madoc. Further lowering and abolition of tariffs led to a market in France and Scandinavia, and the slates went from Hamburg (which remained Port Madoc's major destination) on into central Europe. A less frequent trade meanwhile developed with America.

Ship-building had been traditional in the area since the 18th century, particularly at Pwllheli, where 260 vessels were built between 1759 and 1824. The vast increase in export trade now gave rise to a major ship-building industry at Port Madoc. The techniques used were traditional, and in fact by then old-fashioned — everything was made on the spot by local craftsmen — but the result was remarkably effective. It is generally acknowledged that Port Madoc schooners were of very superior quality (34).

Three-masted vessels, characterised by a slanted bow, with fore-and-aft, rather than square-rigged, sails (which allowed them to beat to windward and thus to be able to make short tacks away from a lee shore beset with obstructions) they were strongly built and more than adequate for the slate trade in which they were mainly employed. It was a form specifically developed to cope with the sudden build-up of short, high waves off the south-Caernarfonshire coast and the strong landward drift of tidal current which made progress hard and hazardous for squatter vessels.

In their last, fully-developed form, a type called Western Ocean Yachts, the schooners reached a peak of refinement, evoking adoring praise from all experts, no less for their beauty and elegance than for their perfection of efficiency.

At a peak in 1873 Port Madoc exported 116,567 tons of slate. A slight lull was followed by a revival in the 1880's, and the early 1890's saw Port Madoc's last and greatest period of ship-building in full flow. The industry then involved the whole town, and the launch of a new schooner was an event which everybody turned out to celebrate. The slate industry declined from 1903, and the schooners largely traded fish and imported commodities from Liverpool and Ireland. Many of the later ships were sold to new owners in Newfoundland, where they ended their days. The German connection continued well into this century, but was brought to an abrupt close, and with it the boom days of Port Madoc, with the start of the Great War in August 1914.

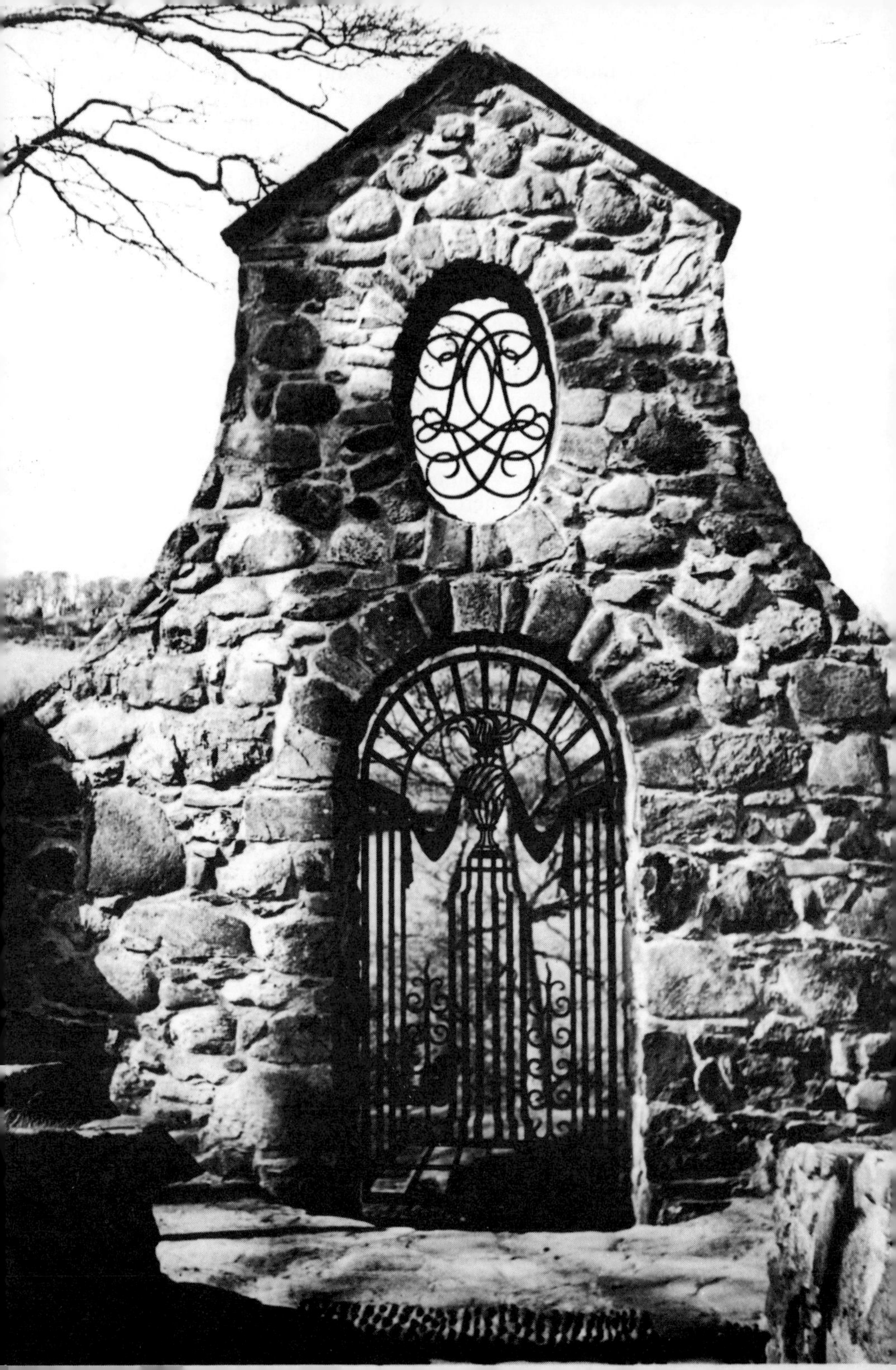

INTO OUR TIMES

THIS area has been rich not only in history but also in personalities who have affected history. Porthmadog would never have had its time of flowering, the impact of which had been felt in places as diverse as Hamburg and Newfoundland, if it had not been for the occurrence there of individuals as remarkable as Madocks and Holland. It is almost incredible that at the same time, the late 19th century, a personality and career was developing only six or so miles away which was to have an influence in an even greater field.

David Lloyd George was not actually born at Llanystumdwy, the village just west of Criccieth, but there and Criccieth were home for him from his infancy until his death, a span of 82 years (35). He was born in 1836 at New York Place, Chorlton-upon-Medlock, Manchester, where a plaque on a nearby house commemmorates this event. His parents were of course Welsh, his father William George a schoolmaster originally from Pembrokeshire, who died when David was only eighteen months old. His mother (nèe Elizabeth Lloyd, the source of his double surname) moved with the child and his elder sister Mary Ellen back to Llanystumdwy where her brother lived, and Lloyd George was brought up in his house.

Richard, 'Uncle Lloyd', was a shoemaker and a part-time Baptist minister, and he evidently had the traditional Welsh respect for education since he coached the young Lloyd George and instilled in him the radical principles which are an essential part of Welsh values. David's formal education was limited to Llanystumdwy village school, which he left at thirteen. Shortly after the family's move a younger brother, William, was born. A plaque now identifies the cottage, across the road from the Feathers Inn, where they lived.

When he was sixteen Lloyd George joined a firm of solicitors in Porthmadog as an articled clerk, and five years later, in 1884 (having passed his law exams), he formed his own practice in Criccieth, later in Porthmadog, and continued as a solicitor in partnership with his brother for the next five years. From the start a dedicated politician, he was elected to the newly-formed Caernarfonshire County Council in 1888, and in that same year gained the nomination to the local Parliamentary seat. In 1890 the death of the conservative member presented him with the opportunity of a by-election. He was twenty-seven when he contested, and won, the seat of Caernarfon Boroughs, by a margin of only eighteen votes.

Lloyd George's interest in politics was primarily nationalistic, and he became a Liberal because the Welsh Nationalists had sided with the Liberal Party in support of their policy of Welsh disestablishment. Lloyd George's nationalistic ambitions at that time went further than this non-conformist aim, since he wanted complete home rule. He was already a founder member of Cymru Fydd, the early form of the present Plaid Cymru,

38. The Lloyd George memorial at Llanystumdwy.

37. Salem chapel.
37. Curnow Vosper's 'Salem'.

INTO OUR TIMES

the nationalist party. Radicalism, nationalism and non-conformity are interlinked, and we have to remember that this is very much a chapel-based area. It is perhaps appropriate that the stereotyped depiction of Welsh tradition, Curnow Vosper's painting 'Salem', is actually based on Salem Chapel in the Nantcol valley behind Llanbedr (37).

Undoubtedly Lloyd George's radical principles had a lasting effect on British politics. He rose from these unpropitious beginnings at Llanystumdwy to become Chancellor of the Exchequer and then Prime Minister, from 1916 to 1922, the time of the First World War and its aftermath. Throughout his renowned career as national leader he remained true to his roots, and he held the same Caernarfon seat for fifty-five years. When illness forced him to retire in 1931 he returned to live in Criccieth, in a house called Bryn Awelon, on the north side of the town, and is buried back at Llanystumdwy, beside the attractive river Dwyfor, near where a memorial museum houses mementoes of his life (38). Two months before he died he resigned his seat to accept a peerage, characteristically taking his title from his home region, Earl Lloyd George of Dwyfor.

During the period of Lloyd George's rise, Porthmadog's decline, and Britain's adjustment to the 20th century and our modern times, Lleyn, like everywhere else, had been slowly changing. Seaside resorts were an invention of the 19th century, a new middle class forming the habit of taking holidays in other parts of their own country, seeking scenery and health-giving seaside air. As Pwllheli declined as a port it rose as a beach resort, served from 1867 by the Cambrian Coast Railway from Barmouth. The beach itself had been improved by the effects of drainage, and its new role had developed fast from the second decade of the 19th century.

Criccieth likewise benefited greatly by the coming of the railway, but their contemporary ancient borough, Nefyn, was deprived of this advantage and left somewhat out on a limb by the eventual rejection of Porth Dinllaen as the port for Ireland. A two-mile stretch of sand at Morfa Nefyn compensates for this isolation, and indeed all down the coast there are justly famous beaches, such as Porth Oer, the 'Whistling Sands' near Aberdaron, Porth Neigwl, known as 'Hell's Mouth', to its east, and on the other side of the peninsula Morfa Bychan near Porthmadog and Black Rock sands.

One of the most successful of these small resorts is undoubtedly Abersoch (39), near the peninsula's eastern tip, sheltered from prevailing winds and intimately enclosed by headlands. Its rise from fishing-village to major yacht harbour is a phenomenon of the last few decades, and it thrives now as a small-boat haven, its main focus being its yacht club.

The area is full of contrasts and surprises, and few ten-mile journeys could include two things so far apart in character as Butlin's holiday camp, east of Pwllheli, and Portmeirion (40) east of Porthmadog. Both cater for residents and visitors, both present a consistent and self-contained

39. Abersoch.
40. Portmeirion

INTO OUR TIMES

world, but there the points of similarity end.

Portmeirion, like so much we have considered in this area, is the result of the determination and creativity of a single forceful individual. The late Sir Clough Williams-Ellis acquired an overgrown headland and started to clear its undergrowth in 1926, having identified its mild climate and secluded position as being the perfect situation for his romantic vision of an ideal village. The land had previously belonged to his uncle, once the site of a small settlement and landscaped with tree-planting and rhododendrons during the mid-19th century.

Sir Clough (who died in 1978 at the age of 94) was a largely self-trained architect, the descendant of Caernarfonshire landowners, who became fashionable and successful in London in the 1920's. His work may be seen in various parts of the country and the world, but particularly in his home area, where his liking for urns and pedestals has left his distinctive mark on the gateways and grounds of many country houses. He it was who designed the grave of Lloyd George at Llanystumdwy (38), bringing together two of the powerful personalities of this area. A man very much in the mould of Madocks, he is rightly described in *The Times*'s obituary as "his own best work".

Having first converted the old house by the sea to a hotel, Williams-Ellis began to collect from various parts of the country interesting and rare buildings, which he had dismantled, transported and re-erected at Portmeirion. The result is a fanciful and amusing world, a total environment intended only to please.

This extraordinary project developed over a span of more than thirty years, the last item (the Colonnade, a structure formerly in Bristol) being added in 1959. Portmeirion has had its times of fame and fashion, most recently when it became nationally known as the location of the television series, 'The Prisoner'. In the pre-war years it was a favourite retreat of the Duke of Windsor, and Noel Coward wrote his play 'Blithe Spirit' there, up in the Watch House, during a single week.

The unexpected is a frequent occurrence in this area as a whole, where a great range of historic land uses is packed into a relatively small mileage. Perhaps this is most striking where it is most directly related to our modern age, as at the nuclear power station which overlooks the lake at Trawsfynydd (41).

Here the outlook is unavoidably contentious. Trawsfynydd was commissioned in 1965, and is now reaching the end of its working life. It may continue in its present form into the 1990's, but by then a decision will have to be made as to its future. One option is its replacement by a newer form, a Pressurised Water Reactor. The power station provides employment for about 600 people, in an area where there are few other sources of employment, and although a new reactor would employ significantly fewer there are local arguments against its complete closure, in spite of the

'Linda' climbing through the Vale of Maentwrog.
41.   Trawsfynydd nuclear power station.

INTO OUR TIMES

presumed danger from pollution to those working there or living nearby. The existing station will in any case have to be 'decommissioned', an enormously expensive process, estimated in this case to cost some £40 million. The problems involved in removing the radioactive material are immense, and as yet untested, since no large reactor has yet been shut down. Its replacement with a Pressurised Water Reactor, though it would mop up some of the resulting unemployment, is a similarly unknown factor, and doubts about the safety of such installations must linger, following the accident at Three Mile Island, in America, in 1979.

Such issues are perhaps not typical of this largely idyllic area, but they are in scale with its strong character and its constant ability to surprise. Indeed to stand on Tomen y Mur, amid the remains of a Roman fort and among the associations of old mythology, and to see on the one hand moorland unchanged since the wizard Gwydion came there, whenever that might have been, and on the other the embodiment of our present uneasy and dangerous times, is to receive a significant shock. This is a land where history is built into the terrain, and it still goes on.

ACKNOWLEDGEMENTS

There are a number of books on specialised aspects of the history of this area which are not only invaluable to anyone studying the subject but also highly enjoyable and greatly to be recommended to the general reader:

Immortal Sails by Henry Hughes give a first-hand account of Porthmadog's maritime history.
Porthmadog Ships by Emrys Hughes and Aled Eames is an expansion by Aled Eames of records made by Emrys Hughes.
Madocks and the Wonder of Wales by Elizabeth Beazley recently re-issued, is a masterly and highly readable biography of Madocks.

PHOTOGRAPHS:
Cambridge University collection of air photographs:
3, 6, 14, 18 (both), 30
E. Emrys Jones, Old Colwyn:
4, 12, 13, 15, 17, 19, 22, 26, 27, 28, 31, 33, 38, 37 (both), 39, 40, 41
National Monuments Record for Wales:
9, 16, 20 (both)
Author:
14, 16 (inset), 21, 27, 29, 30
Gwynedd Archives Service:
34, 32, 36
Ffestiniog Narrow Gauge Railway:
Photograph on page 50
Gwasg Carreg Gwalch:
5

Michael Senior is also the author of 'The Conwy Valley — its long history', 'Llandudno's Story', 'Anglesey, The Island's Story' and similar booklets on Caernarfon and Conwy, as well as 'Portrait of North Wales', now available in paperback.